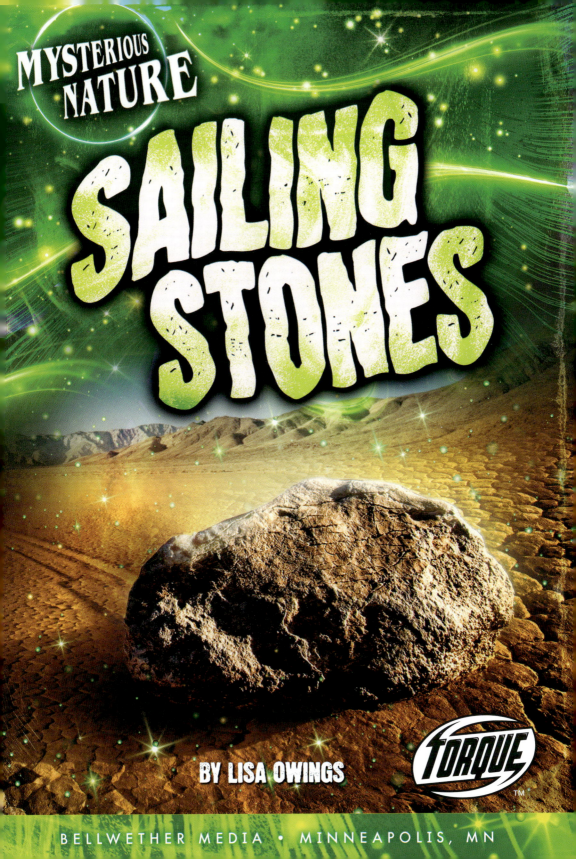

Torque brims with excitement perfect for thrill-seekers of all kinds. Discover daring survival skills, explore uncharted worlds, and marvel at mighty engines and extreme sports. In *Torque* books, anything can happen. Are you ready?

This edition first published in 2025 by Bellwether Media, Inc.

No part of this publication may be reproduced in whole or in part without written permission of the publisher. For information regarding permission, write to Bellwether Media, Inc., Attention: Permissions Department, 6012 Blue Circle Drive, Minnetonka, MN 55343.

Library of Congress Cataloging-in-Publication Data

LC record for Sailing Stones available at: https://lccn.loc.gov/2024009427

Text copyright © 2025 by Bellwether Media, Inc. TORQUE and associated logos are trademarks and/or registered trademarks of Bellwether Media, Inc. Bellwether Media is a division of Chrysalis Education Group.

Editor: Rebecca Sabelko   Designer: Josh Brink

Printed in the United States of America, North Mankato, MN.

TABLE OF CONTENTS

TRAILS IN THE SAND	4
WHAT ARE SAILING STONES?	6
A ROCKY ROAD TO ANSWERS	10
A RARE EVENT	14
GLOSSARY	22
TO LEARN MORE	23
INDEX	24

Trails in the Sand

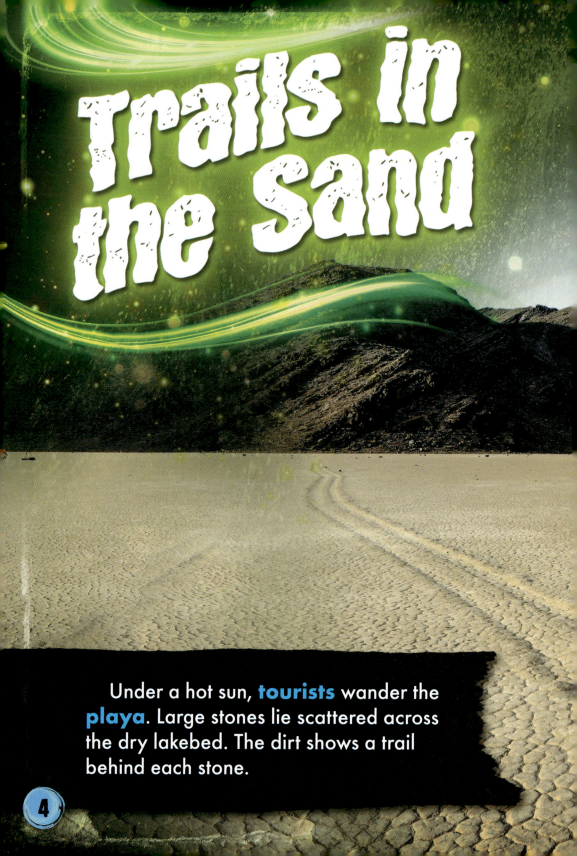

Under a hot sun, **tourists** wander the **playa**. Large stones lie scattered across the dry lakebed. The dirt shows a trail behind each stone.

It looks like the stones have dragged themselves across the playa. But how? Tourists stare at the stones. Will the stones move?

What Are Sailing Stones?

Sailing stones are rocks that appear to have moved by themselves. They leave long trails across dry, smooth lakebeds. The best place to see them is Racetrack Playa in Death Valley, California.

HOW HEAVY?

Some sailing stones weigh up to 700 pounds (318 kilograms). That is about the size of a large grizzly bear!

Sailing stones can weigh hundreds of pounds. Yet some have sailed hundreds of feet. For decades, visitors and scientists puzzled over the mystery of how the stones move.

Very few people have seen sailing stones move. Scientists believe the stones only move once every five or ten years. Trails were the only **evidence** of the movements for many years.

Birthing Stones

 Where? Freita Mountain, Portugal

 What happens? Smaller "baby" stones found inside large "mother" rocks fall out when the mother rock is worn away by wind and rain.

So far, sailing stones have mainly been studied in and around Death Valley. The area's landscape and weather make this **phenomenon** possible.

A Rocky Road to Answers

Sailing stones were first **observed** in the early 1900s. Scientists have been curious about them ever since. Some thought strong winds moved the stones.

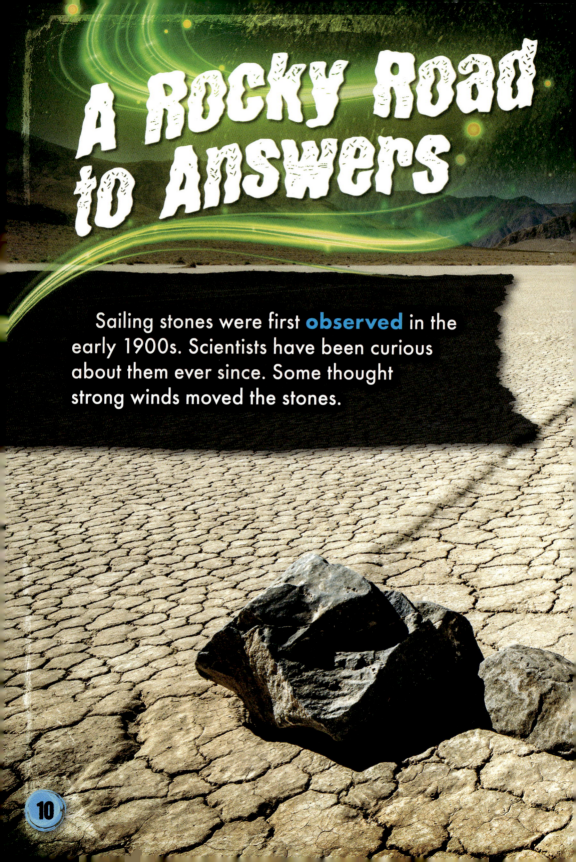

Pulled by Magnets

Earth's magnetic field

Idea: Earth's magnetic field moves the stones.

Disproved: The stones do not have any magnetic metals in them.

Some people guessed **magnetic fields** could be the cause. Others suggested **earthquakes** or changes in **gravity** caused movements. A few people wondered if aliens had moved the stones!

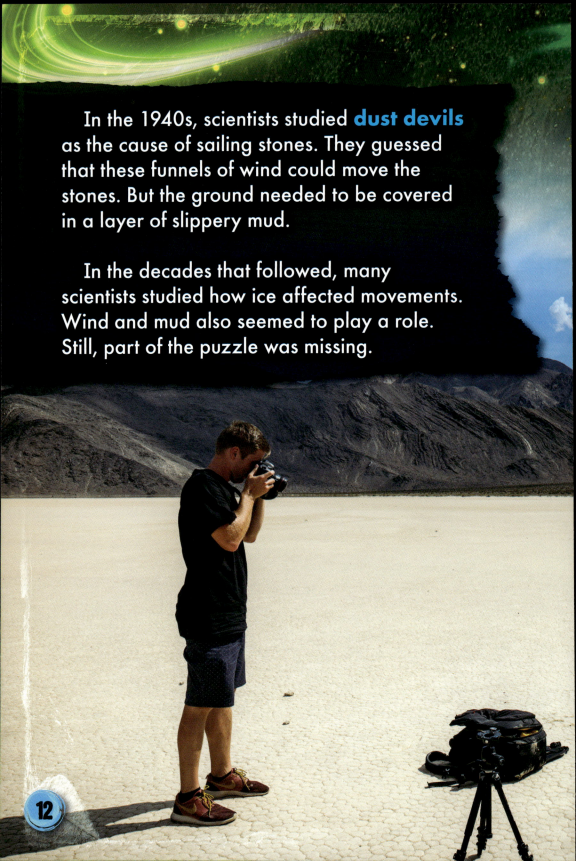

In the 1940s, scientists studied **dust devils** as the cause of sailing stones. They guessed that these funnels of wind could move the stones. But the ground needed to be covered in a layer of slippery mud.

In the decades that followed, many scientists studied how ice affected movements. Wind and mud also seemed to play a role. Still, part of the puzzle was missing.

dust devil

MISCHIEF ON THE PLAYA?

Some people thought people or animals were moving the rocks. But there were no footprints or animal tracks to support this.

A Rare Event

In the 2010s, a team of scientists from California put **GPS trackers** on 15 stones. They also set up **time-lapse** cameras. These technologies helped the scientists observe and understand the stones' movements.

First Sighting

 When? December 20, 2013

 Where? Racetrack Playa, Death Valley, California

 What happened? A team of scientists were the first to see sailing stones move. More than 60 rocks sailed!

The team saw the stones sail in person in the winter of 2013. The last piece of the puzzle finally fell into place!

The scientists arrived in Death Valley in late December. Around 3 inches (7 centimeters) of rainwater covered the playa. The water froze overnight. The next day, the ice began to melt and break apart.

rainwater covering the playa

Soon, there were thin sheets of ice. They floated on the water's surface. A gentle wind blew the ice sheets across the playa.

The ice sheets pushed the stones. The stones left trails in the dirt as they moved.

How Stones Sail

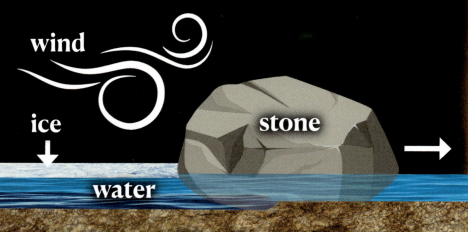

The team of scientists noticed the rocks moved very slowly. Rough stones tended to move in straight lines. Smooth stones left wandering trails. Rocks near each other often had trails of the same length and shape.

Sailing stones only move under perfect conditions. The rocks must be partly above water. The ice sheets must be strong yet thin. The wind must be gentle and steady.

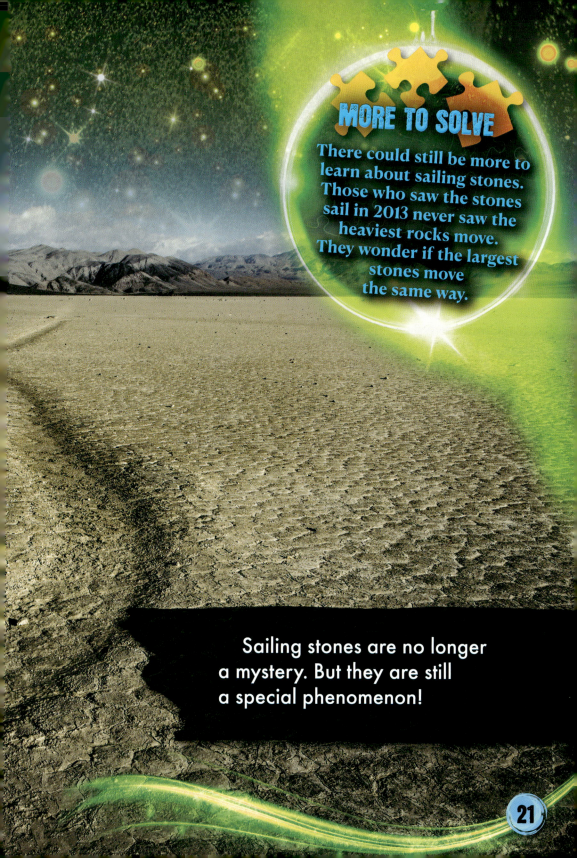

MORE TO SOLVE

There could still be more to learn about sailing stones. Those who saw the stones sail in 2013 never saw the heaviest rocks move. They wonder if the largest stones move the same way.

Sailing stones are no longer a mystery. But they are still a special phenomenon!

GLOSSARY

dust devils—whirlwinds that carry sand and dust

earthquakes—events in which the ground shakes from the movement of Earth's crust

evidence—information that helps prove or disprove something

GPS trackers—devices that use information from satellites to keep track of the location of something

gravity—the force that pulls objects toward one another

magnetic fields—areas of space around magnetic objects in which magnetic forces can be detected

observed—looked closely at something

phenomenon—an event or fact that can be seen or felt

playa—the flat bottom of a desert lakebed; playas are mostly dry but at times fill with water.

time-lapse—related to photos or images that are taken at slow speeds but viewed at fast speeds

tourists—people who travel to visit a place

TO LEARN MORE

AT THE LIBRARY

Maloney, Brenna. *Desert*. New York, N.Y.: Children's Press, 2024.

Quick, Megan. *Do You Dare Visit Death Valley?* Buffalo, N.Y.: Enslow Publishing, 2024.

Rathburn, Betsy. *Rock Crafts*. Minneapolis, Minn.: Bellwether Media, 2020.

ON THE WEB

Factsurfer.com gives you a safe, fun way to find more information.

1. Go to www.factsurfer.com

2. Enter "sailing stones" into the search box and click 🔍.

3. Select your book cover to see a list of related content.

INDEX

aliens, 11
animals, 13
birthing stones, 8
California, 6, 14
cameras, 14
Death Valley, 6, 9, 16
dust devils, 12, 13
earthquakes, 11
explanation, 14, 15, 16, 17, 18, 19, 20
first sighting, 14
GPS trackers, 14
gravity, 11
history, 10, 11, 12, 13, 14, 15, 16, 21

how stones sail, 18
ice, 12, 16, 17, 18, 20
lakebed, 4, 6
magnetic fields, 11
mud, 12
playa, 4, 5, 6, 16, 17
Racetrack Playa, 6
rocks, 6, 13, 19, 20, 21
size, 6, 7
tourists, 4, 5
trail, 4, 6, 8, 18, 19
water, 16, 17, 20
winds, 10, 12, 17, 20

The images in this book are reproduced through the courtesy of: BiniClick, front cover (hero); pabradyphoto, front cover (background); Bill45, pp. 2-3, 22-24; Luckyphotography, pp. 4-5; davidchoophotography, pp. 6-7; Aija Repsa, p. 8 (birthing stones); Paul Brady/ Alamy, pp. 8-9; Vezzani Photography, pp. 10-11; Designua, p. 11 (pulled by magnets); Oscity, pp. 12-13; totajila, p. 13 (dust devil); Carver Mostardi/ Alamy, pp. 14-15; Cody Duncan/ Alamy, pp. 16-17; Mike Hartmann/ PLOS, p. 17; KingVector, p. 18 (stone); Amar and Isabelle Guillen - Guillen Photo LLC/ Alamy, pp. 18-19; Jeff Stamer, pp. 20-21; Paul Brady Photography, back cover.